Mmm... bacon.

Love,

Caitlin Ross

P.S- We're proud ot you and stuff :)

RECIPES

Every Man Should Know

This book is for hungry guys.

Copyright © 2010 by Quirk Productions, Inc.

All rights reserved. No part of this book may be reproduced in any form without written permission from the publisher.

Library of Congress Cataloging in Publication Number: 2010925786

ISBN: 978-1-59474-474-7

Printed in Malaysia

Typeset in Goudy and Monotype Old Style

Designed by Jenny Kraemer
Illustrations by Kate Francis

Production management by John J. McGurk
Editorial assistance by Jane Morley and Alexandra Bitzer

Lobster with Beer and Butter Sauce (page 100) thanks to Rick Ford, a man who knows his crustaceans.

10 9 8 7 6 5 4 3 2

Quirk Books
215 Church Street
Philadelphia, PA 19106
www.quirkbooks.com

RECIPES

Every Man Should Know

By Susan Russo and Brett Cohen

QUIRK BOOKS

PHILADELPHIA

Introduction

So, why should men cook?

1. Women think men who cook are sexy.
2. It involves fire, sharp instruments, and meat.
3. Women think men who cook are sexy, and it involves, fire, sharp instruments, and meat.

We can't imagine you need more reasons than those. But heck, we've got more reasons anyway.

4. Home cooking is cheaper than eating out, which means more money for other stuff.
5. It's just as tasty and less fatty than eating out all the time, which means it keeps you happier longer.
6. If you can cook for friends—while tailgating, at a barbecue, for DVD/poker/videogame night— they will worship you and call you the man. (And they will buy the drinks.)

Here, finally, is a book of the absolute essential recipes every guy should know. This little black book is full of the basic recipes and techniques to get you started in the kitchen, and it offers some great variations to impress friends, family, and the ladies. We tell you which pots and pans to buy, what's the difference between slicing and dicing, and how many pints are in a quart. (Two.) We give you awesome sandwiches for a man-sized hunger—and an easy guide to making her a romantic breakfast in bed.

Basically, this book has got your back. Plus, it's small enough to fit in your back pocket, so you will never ever need to write a grocery list again. Congratulations, Sir, on becoming a modern-day Renaissance man.

Kitchen Tools

Navigating the kitchen is as easy as, well, pie. But only if you have the right equipment. These basic tools won't let you down.

Slicing and Dicing*

a. 1 8- to 10-inch chef's knife (meat, vegetables, mincing)

b. 1 8- to 10-inch serrated knife (breads, pizza, pies, tomatoes)

c. 1 3½- to 5-inch paring knife (peeling and cutting small fruits and vegetables)

d. 1 knife sharpener

e. 1 vegetable peeler

f. 2 plastic cutting boards (one for meat only)

g. 1 wooden cutting board

---

* **Note:** Never place good knives in the dishwasher. Sharpen them frequently for optimal slicing and dicing.

Prepping

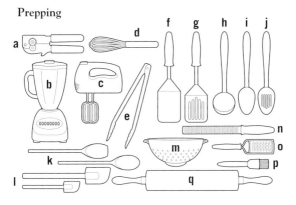

a. 1 can opener

b. 1 blender

c. 1 electric hand mixer

d. 1 whisk

e. 1 pair tongs

f. 1 flexible spatula

g. 1 nonflexible spatula

h. 1 ladle

i. 1 large spoon

j. 1 slotted spoon

k. 2 wooden spoons, one with a flatter top

l. 2 rubber spatulas, small and large

m. 1 colander

n. 1 microplane grater for zesting

o. 1 cheese grater
p. 1 heatproof brush for olive oil and marinades
q. 1 rolling pin

Measuring

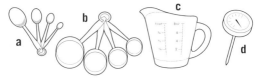

a. 1 set measuring spoons
b. 1 set dry-ingredient measuring cups
c. 1 liquid measuring cup
d. 1 instant-read meat thermometer

Cooking and Baking

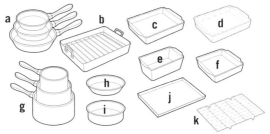

a. 3 nonstick skillets/frying pans: 8-, 10-, and 12-inch
b. 1 roasting pan with rack

c. 1 9-by-13-inch baking pan

d. 1 glass or ceramic 9-by-13-inch baking dish

e. 1 8-by-4-inch loaf pan

f. 1 8- or 9-inch square baking pan

g. 3 saucepans: 1½ quart, 3 or 4 quart, and 4½ to 5 quart

h. 1 9-inch pie plate

i. 2 9-inch round cake pans

j. 2 large, heavy baking sheets

k. 2 wire cooling racks

Serving and Storing

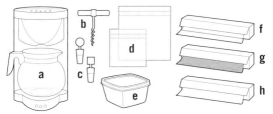

a. 1 coffeepot

b. 1 corkscrew

c. 2 bottle stoppers

d. Large and small zip-top plastic bags

e. Airtight plastic containers

f. Plastic wrap

g. Aluminum foil

h. Parchment paper

Cooking Terms

U nderstanding these basic cooking terms takes the
mystery out of any recipe.

Boil: Heat liquid until bubbles form on the surface.

Broil: Cook food quickly by placing it directly under
or above high heat, either just under the heat
source in the oven or just over the fire on the grill.

Chop: Cut food into medium, irregular pieces.

Combine: Stir ingredients together until the mixture
doesn't separate.

Cube: Cut food into uniform pieces, about ½ to ¾
inch around.

Dice: Cut food into small uniform pieces, about ⅛ to
¼ inch around.

Dredge: Before cooking, coat a food in ingredients
such as egg, bread crumbs, or flour.

Flake: Break off small pieces or layers of food with
a utensil, typically a fork.

Fold: Gently combine a lighter ingredient into a
heavier one by drawing a rubber spatula through
the middle of the bowl, underneath ingredients,
and up the side of the bowl; repeat while rotating
the bowl a bit with each fold, until ingredients
are combined.

Fry: Cook over direct heat in fat (used for onion rings, chicken wings).

Mince: Cut food into the tiniest pieces possible.

Panfry: Cooking food quickly in a hot pan with a fat, such as oil or butter; similar to sautéing, but generally uses more fat and creates more browning (used for fish, pork chops, steak).

Parboil: Boil to partially cook and finish cooking later.

Puree: Blend food in a blender or food processor until smooth and creamy (as for mashed potatoes, margaritas).

Sauté: Cook food quickly in a hot pan with a small amount of fat, such as oil or butter.

Sear: Quickly brown or char food over very high heat (used for meats).

Simmer: Cook over low heat; bubbling slightly, but not boiling.

Slice: Cut food into strips.

Chapter 1

Hearty Breakfast Classics

A Great Cup of Joe

Y ou don't need a fancy barista degree to brew really good coffee. Just keep these tips in mind.

- **Start with an automatic-drip coffeemaker.** It's low-maintenance and easy to clean. For optimal flavor, use either a reusable gold mesh filter (available online, at coffee shops, or at kitchen-goods stores) or brown, unbleached paper filters.

- **Use freshly ground coffee beans instead of instant.** Try different roasts—light, medium, dark—to find the one you prefer. Also, make sure the coffee is ground according to the type of filter used in your coffeemaker.

- **Pick one coffee scoop and stick with it.** That way, you'll know exactly how much coffee to use each time. Start by using ¼ cup ground coffee to 4 cups water, and adjust according to your taste. Brew only as much coffee as you need; coffee that sits in a pot too long will burn and taste bitter.

Eggs

5 to 35
minutes

1
serving

If you wake up on the wrong side of the bed, it's easy to set things right with a good breakfast.

> *"Nothing helps scenery like bacon and eggs."*
> —Mark Twain

Fried Eggs: Add 2 to 3 teaspoons olive oil to a small skillet over medium-low heat. Crack an egg in a small bowl or glass. Slide egg into pan. Add another, if desired. Cook undisturbed until the white is firm. Slide onto a plate. Season with salt and pepper, and serve hot.

Hard-Boiled Eggs: Place large eggs in a single layer in a saucepan and just cover with water. Bring water to a boil over high heat for one minute. Remove pan from heat, cover, and let sit 15 minutes. Transfer eggs to a bowl of cold water. After 10 minutes, remove eggs and tap against the countertop to crack. Remove peel under gently running water. Store in an airtight container in the fridge up to 5 days.

Scrambled Eggs: Crack 3 large eggs in a bowl. Add 2 tablespoons milk or cream, salt, and pepper. Whisk until blended. Add 2 to 3 teaspoons butter to a small nonstick skillet over medium-high heat. Add eggs and let cook, untouched, 15 to 20 seconds. Continue to cook 1 to 1½ minutes, gently stirring several times with a wooden spoon or rubber spatula. Serve hot.

Sausage-and-Egg Breakfast Hash

| **15**
minutes | **6** to **8**
servings |

There's no better way to start the day than with all your favorite breakfast foods—eggs, sausage, potatoes, cheese, hot sauce—together in one glorious, piping hot dish.

3 tablespoons butter

1 yellow onion, diced

1 green or red bell pepper, diced

4 chicken-apple sausage links (about 10 ounces), cooked and sliced

3 cups peeled, shredded potatoes (about 3 potatoes) or 3 cups frozen hash browns

1 dozen eggs

Salt and freshly ground black pepper

1 cup shredded cheddar cheese

Several dashes hot sauce

1. Melt butter in a large skillet over medium-high heat. Add onions and peppers and cook 5 minutes. Add sausage and cook 3 minutes. Add potatoes and cook another 7 to 8 minutes, stirring occasionally, until golden brown.

2. In a large bowl, beat together eggs, salt, and pepper; pour into skillet. Cook 3 to 4 minutes, stirring frequently. Add cheese and hot sauce. Cook until eggs are just set (no longer runny) and cheese is melted, about 1 to 2 minutes. Serve hot.

Better-Than-IHOP Pancakes

25	10
minutes	*servings*

Nothing says lazy Sunday morning better than a tall stack of fluffy, tender pancakes doused with warm maple syrup. Whether you make them from scratch with this simple recipe or use a box mix, it's easy to take pancakes to the next level with tasty add-ins and toppings like chocolate chips, cinnamon-sugar apples, and golden rum bananas.

1½ cups all-purpose flour

2 tablespoons sugar

1 tablespoon baking powder

½ teaspoon salt

1 cup whole milk or buttermilk

2 eggs

½ teaspoon vanilla extract, optional

Maple syrup and melted butter for serving

1. In a mixing bowl, whisk together flour, sugar, baking powder, and salt. In another bowl, whisk together milk, eggs, and vanilla extract (if using). Add dry ingredients to wet, and whisk until just combined. It's OK if batter is a little lumpy. Let it rest 10 to 15 minutes.

2. Heat a large frying pan or griddle over medium-high heat. Splash it with a few drops of water: When they pop and jump, you're good to go. Lightly grease pan with butter. Pour batter by the quarter-cupful onto pan, being careful not to overcrowd if cooking more than one at a time. Leave each pancake alone until edges start to turn golden and little bubbles form on top. Then, using a spatula, give it a quick, steady flip. (Remember, the first two or three are for the dog.) Cook 30 to 60 seconds more, or until puffed up and golden brown.

3. Repeat with remaining batter, adding butter to the pan as necessary. Serve pancakes right away, or keep in a warm oven (250°F) until you're ready to eat. Top with warm maple syrup and melted butter.

Here are a few simple pancake variations; classic toppings follow on page 26.

Chocolate-Chip Pancakes: After pouring pancakes into the pan, sprinkle a few chocolate chips or peanut butter chips over the top.

Berry Pancakes: Once pancakes are poured, sprinkle with a few fresh berries or unthawed frozen berries. Serve with warm maple syrup or honey.

Kid-Friendly: Shaped like an elephant, a dog, or a mouse, these pancakes are guaranteed to get a smile. Pour about ¼ cup batter into the pan. Wait a minute, then add ⅛ cup batter twice to make two ears; make sure they overlap the center pancake so they'll stick together. M&Ms, bananas, and sliced strawberries make great eyes and noses. When you're done, drizzle chocolate syrup to make a mouth.

Pancake Sandwiches: Fill two pancakes with eggs and bacon, cream cheese and jam, or PB&J.

Tasty Pancake Toppings

Sugar and Berries and other decadent toppings are a quick and easy way to fortify everyday pancakes for a special brunch or a romantic breakfast in bed.

Bananas and Honey: Cook sliced bananas in a buttered pan until golden. Top with a dash of cinnamon, a drizzle of honey, and a few chopped walnuts or pecans.

Maple Apples: Cook sliced apples in butter until soft. Sprinkle with a little cinnamon and brown sugar. Drizzle with maple syrup.

Rum Bananas with Nuts: Cook sliced bananas in a little butter and a splash of rum for a few minutes; spoon over pancakes and sprinkle with walnuts.

Sugar and Berries: Place a cup of fresh berries in a bowl with a little sugar and toss. Spoon over pancakes, and dust with powdered sugar.

Cinnamon-Sugar Apples: Cook sliced apples or pears in a little butter and sprinkle with cinnamon, brown sugar, and raisins.

The Hangover Cure

5	1
minutes	*serving*

Yup. It happened again. Allow yourself exactly 3 minutes of self-loathing and then move on . . .

1 tall glass cold water

1 tall glass cold seltzer water mixed with orange juice and a splash of cranberry juice, or whatever juice you've got in the fridge

A few pats butter

2 to 3 eggs, lightly beaten

A couple handfuls salty tortilla chips, scavenged from the remains of last night's party; avoid ones smeared with remnants of dip (or break off the good parts, if you're really desperate)

As much cheddar cheese as you want

As much hot sauce as you want

1. Rehydrate yourself first with water, then with seltzer and juice.

2. Add butter to a medium skillet over medium heat. Add eggs to skillet. Cook halfway through and then add chips,

cheese, and hot sauce. Continue to cook until eggs are set.

3. Pour yourself a mug of strong, hot coffee. Eat.

Fool-Proof French Toast

20
minutes

8
slices

Thick slices of French toast taste great with warm butter and maple syrup poured overtop (both microwaved a few seconds before serving) and dusted with powdered sugar. Even better, try flavorful toppings such as almonds, cinnamon-sugar, and maple bacon.

6 eggs

1½ cups whole or low-fat milk

¾ teaspoon ground cinnamon

1½ teaspoons vanilla extract

Zest of 1 large orange, optional

1 pat butter

8 slices Texas toast (thickly sliced challah bread works well, too)

Warm butter, maple syrup, or powdered sugar for topping

1. In a shallow bowl or pie plate, lightly whisk eggs; add milk, cinnamon, vanilla, and orange zest (if using) and whisk to combine.

2. Place a skillet over medium-low heat. Melt butter in skillet until just coated.

3. Dip one bread slice in egg mixture, allowing excess to drip into bowl. Add to skillet and cook about 1 minute per side, or until bread is golden brown and egg has set. Transfer to a warm plate and cover until ready to serve. Repeat with remaining slices, buttering skillet as necessary.

Almond-Crusted French Toast: After dredging each slice in egg, dip in sliced almonds until coated on both sides. Serve topped with fresh berries and powdered sugar.

Cinnamon-Sugar French Toast: Mix 1 cup sugar with 1 tablespoon cinnamon. After dredging each slice in egg, dredge in cinnamon-sugar.

Golden Nut-and-Fruit French Toast: Sauté sliced apples, bananas, peaches, or pears in a little butter until tender. Season with cinnamon and sugar, and add a few nuts. Scatter over French toast.

Maple-Bacon and Banana French Toast: Cook maple-smoked bacon strips until crispy. Sauté sliced bananas in a little butter until tender and sprinkle with cinnamon. Scatter over French toast and drizzle with maple syrup.

French Toast Sandwiches: Before (or after) grilling, fill two slices with peanut butter and jelly, Nutella and sliced strawberries, or ham and cheese.

Breakfast Burritos

15	4	2
minutes	burritos	servings

For a hungry-man breakfast, burritos never let you down and are easy and adaptable. You can make beef or shredded-pork breakfast burritos, toss in vegetables like beans and red bell peppers, or add extra cheese.

1 tablespoon olive oil, divided

½ pound hot sausage, such as chorizo, casing removed

6 large eggs, lightly beaten

Salt and black pepper to taste

4 (8-inch) flour tortillas

½ cup shredded sharp cheddar or Monterey Jack cheese

¼ cup of your favorite salsa

2 scallions, thinly sliced

Flesh of 1 ripe avocado, thinly sliced

Sour cream, hot sauce, and lime wedges for serving

1. In a frying pan over medium heat, warm 2 teaspoons olive oil. Add sausage and cook 5 minutes, stirring occasionally. Set aside.

2. Next, in a small bowl, whisk together eggs, salt, and pepper. Warm remaining teaspoon olive oil in a small skillet over medium heat, add eggs, and scramble 1 to 2 minutes, or until cooked through but still soft.

3. Place tortillas in a warm skillet, one at a time, and heat 1 minute per side. Place each tortilla on a plate. In a strip down the middle of each tortilla, add sausage, eggs, cheese, salsa, scallions, and avocado slices. Tuck in the end of each tortilla and fold over the sides. Eat 'em while they're hot!

Chapter 2

Sandwiches, Burgers & Snacks

Eight Essential Sandwiches

| 5 to 30 |
| *minutes* |

Sandwiches are easy, filling, and cheap. But most important, they dirty very few dishes.

The Elvis: Spread peanut butter (the King preferred smooth) onto white bread. Add sliced banana and cooked bacon. Close sandwich and panfry with a pat of butter until golden. Eat it while it's hot. The King washed his down with a glass of buttermilk. *Makes 1.*

Philly Cheesesteak: Heat 2 tablespoons olive oil in a large skillet over medium heat. Sauté 1 sliced yellow onion, 1 sliced green bell pepper, and 2 cups sliced mushrooms for 5 minutes; add about 1 pound thinly sliced rib-eye steak (or top sirloin or round) and season with salt and pepper. Cook 5 minutes or until brown and tender. Scoop into hoagie rolls and top with cheese: American, provolone, or Cheez Whiz. Eat it while it's hot. *Makes 4.*

Chicken Cheesesteak: Substitute boneless, skinless chicken breast for the steak. Add Swiss cheese. *Makes 4.*

Peppers and Egg Sandwich: Slice 2 (6-inch) hoagie or torpedo rolls lengthwise without cutting all the way through. Drizzle inside of rolls with olive oil. Broil 2 minutes or until golden. Whisk 6 eggs with salt and black pepper. Warm 2 teaspoons olive oil in a medium skillet over medium heat. Sauté 1 teaspoon minced garlic and 1 medium sliced yellow onion for 1 to 2 minutes. Add 1 sliced green bell pepper and sauté 5 minutes or until soft. Add eggs. Stirring occasionally, cook 2 to 3 minutes or until eggs are set. Put 2 slices mozzarella or provolone cheese in each roll. Top with eggs. Serve hot. *Makes 2.*

Tuna Sandwich: In a bowl, mix 1 (6-ounce) can chunk light or chunk white tuna packed in water (or oil), drained and flaked into chunks with a fork, with ½ cup finely chopped celery, 2 tablespoons finely chopped scallions or chives, ⅓ to ½ cup mayonnaise, 1½ teaspoons Dijon mustard, 2 tablespoons sweet relish, 2 teaspoons lemon juice, and a pinch of salt and black pepper. Spread tuna on buttered, toasted bread; add sliced tomatoes and lettuce. *Makes 2.*

Italian Hero: Whisk 2 teaspoons extra-virgin olive oil, 1 teaspoon balsamic vinegar, and a pinch of salt and pepper. Drizzle half on the inside of a roll and top with mayonnaise. Layer a couple slices each of Italian deli meats, such as soppressata (Italian dried sausage), prosciutto, and mortadella. Add a couple slices buffalo mozzarella. Top with onion slices, shredded lettuce, tomato slices, a few pepperoncini peppers, and 4 fresh basil leaves (if desired). Drizzle with remaining oil-vinegar mixture. *Makes 1*.

Sloppy Joe: Warm 2 tablespoons olive oil in a large skillet over medium heat. Sauté 1 cup finely chopped yellow onion, ½ cup finely diced celery, and ½ cup finely chopped green pepper 2 to 3 minutes, or until just tender. Add 1½ pounds ground beef, stirring to break it up. Cook 10 to 12 minutes, or until browned. Drain off excess fat. Add 1½ to 2 cups tomato sauce (more or less, depending on your desired level of sloppiness), ½ cup ketchup, ¼ cup light brown sugar, 2 tablespoons Worcestershire sauce, 2 teaspoons Tabasco sauce, and 1½ tablespoons red wine vinegar. Simmer uncovered 15 to 20 minutes, or until mixture is thick and a little sloppy but not too soupy. Spoon onto hamburger buns. Eat right away so they don't become Soggy Joes. *Makes 6*.

Shrimp Po'boy: Fill a small, deep pot with at least 2 inches canola oil and heat to 350°F. (If you don't have a thermometer, drop a bit of batter into the hot oil; if it sizzles and bubbles form around it, the oil is ready.) Peel and devein 1½ to 2 pounds extra-large shrimp (about 2 dozen). Rinse and pat dry. In a small bowl, whisk together 1 large egg, ⅓ cup milk, 2 teaspoons hot sauce, and a pinch of salt. In another bowl, mix ½ cup flour, 1 cup cornmeal, and 2 tablespoons Old Bay seasoning.* Add cornmeal to a third bowl. Dredge one shrimp at a time in egg mixture, then flour, then cornmeal until completely coated. Place on a large plate until ready to fry. Fry shrimp in small batches 1 to 2 minutes, or until golden and crisp. Place on a paper-towel-lined plate until ready to eat. Slice rolls open and add lettuce, tomato slices, and shrimp. Drizzle with melted butter and a few dashes of hot sauce. *Makes 4.*

---

* **Note:** You can buy Old Bay seasoning in the spice or seafood section of most major supermarkets.

Grilled Vegetables

15	30	10 to 15	4
minutes for prep	minutes for marinating	minutes for grilling	servings

G rilling isn't just for meat. It also makes vegetables tender and smoky.

"Primarily, I am a meat man, although once in a while I toy with a few vegetables."

—Nat King Cole

Marinade:

¼ cup olive oil

¼ cup balsamic vinegar

½ teaspoon crushed red pepper flakes

¼ teaspoon salt

Vegetables:

2 red bell peppers, cut into 2-inch strips

1 eggplant, cut into ½-inch-thick slices

1 zucchini, cut into ½-inch-thick slices

1 summer squash, cut into ½-inch-thick slices

1 bunch scallions

1 bunch asparagus
Handful torn basil leaves

1. Whisk marinade ingredients together in a bowl. Transfer to a plastic container or zip-top bag and add vegetables. Shake well. Marinate 30 to 45 minutes. Drain.

2. Preheat grill to medium-high and lightly oil grates so that vegetables don't stick. Grill 5 to 6 minutes per side for thicker vegetables and 3 to 4 minutes for scallions and asparagus, or until tender and lightly charred. Garnish with basil, and serve.

Perfect Burgers

5	6 to 8
minutes for prep	minutes for grilling

Here are few key techniques for grilling or panfrying this iconic American food to perfection. Top juicy burgers with good melting cheese—such as American, cheddar, or Swiss—fresh lettuce, tomato, and onion, plus pickles, mustard and ketchup, or relish and mayo.

½ pound ground chuck per person
¼ teaspoon each salt and pepper per pound
   of ground chuck

1. The best burger meat is fresh (not frozen) ground chuck that has 15% to 20% fat. Anything leaner, and you'll sacrifice flavor.

2. Get the grill fired up well before you cook the burgers.

3. Season the beef with a little salt and pepper. If you want, you can add other seasonings, like chopped fresh herbs and/or minced onions. Gently and quickly form ½-pound patties with your hands. (Overhandling meat

makes it less juicy.) Gently press the middle of each patty with your fingertips to flatten it like a puck.

4. Cook 3 to 4 minutes; flip and cook another 3 to 4 minutes for medium-rare. Resist the urge to squish burgers flat with a spatula: All the juices will flow right out. Cook meat shorter or longer to suit your taste, though for maximum safety an internal temperature of 160°F is recommended.

Panfried Burgers: Warm about 1 tablespoon canola oil in a large, heavy skillet. Add patties and, over medium-high heat, cook 3 to 4 minutes, or until browned. Flip and cook 2 to 3 more minutes.

Burger Toppings

It's hard to go wrong with these classic burger fixins.

- BBQ sauce, bacon, and cheddar
- Chili and cheddar
- Avocado, salsa, and Monterey Jack
- Mushrooms, onions, and Swiss
- Caramelized onions and blue cheese
- Fried egg
- Chili, coleslaw, and onions
- Cheddar, avocado, and jalapeño
- Canadian bacon and pineapple rings
- Guacamole, salsa, and sour cream
- Swiss cheese, caramelized onions, and horseradish sauce
- Crispy pancetta, roasted peppers, and mozzarella
- Potato chips, American cheese, mustard, and ketchup
- Onion rings, BBQ sauce, and bacon
- Feta cheese, black olives, pepperoncini, and onions
- Pizza sauce, mozzarella, and pepperoni

Baja-Style Fish Tacos

30	4
minutes	*servings*

Y ou can't make fish tacos for one. It's just not right. They've gotta be eaten in good company and with good beer. So have the guys over: You do the grilling; they do the assembling.

Fish:
4 (6- to 8-ounce) mahimahi fillets
Olive oil
Salt and freshly ground black pepper
Juice of 1 lime

Avocado Sauce:
Flesh of 2 medium-ripe avocados
Juice of 1 lime
Handful fresh cilantro leaves
Pinch cayenne pepper

Tangy Mayo Sauce:
½ cup mayonnaise
1 teaspoon white vinegar
1½ tablespoons water

10 to 12 (6-inch) soft flour tortillas
1 small head cabbage, shredded
2 medium tomatoes, diced
4 scallions, thinly sliced

1. Preheat grill to high. Drizzle fish on both sides with olive oil and sprinkle with salt and pepper. Grill 5 to 7 minutes per side, or until opaque. Remove from heat and drizzle with lime juice.

2. In a small food processor or blender, process avocado, lime juice, cilantro, and cayenne until smooth, with the consistency of thick cream. (Add water to thin, if necessary.) Transfer to a bowl and set aside.

3. In a small bowl, mix mayonnaise and white vinegar. Slowly mix in as much water as needed to make mixture thick and creamy.

4. Place tortillas on top grill rack and heat through, 30 to 60 seconds. Arrange food on a table for self-service. To assemble, hold a tortilla in your hand and spread a spoonful of avocado sauce on it. Add some fish and drizzle with tangy mayo sauce. Top with cabbage, tomatoes, and scallions.

Quick-and-Easy Quesadillas

<10	1
minutes	quesadilla

Cheese quesadillas are delicious, but you can also add fillings such as shredded cooked chicken or pork, refried beans, onions, hot peppers, or spicy black bean dip (page 113). Cut crispy, hot quesadillas into 2 wedges and serve with salsa, guacamole, and sour cream.

Canola or peanut oil for frying, about 1 to 2 teaspoons
2 (8- or 10-inch) flour tortillas
½ cup shredded cheese, such as cheddar or
    Monterey Jack
Fillings of your choice

1. In a large skillet over medium-high heat, add canola oil. Place an 8 or 10-inch round flour tortilla in skillet, and sprinkle with half the cheese. Add fillings and sprinkle with remaining cheese.

2. Fold tortilla in half, tucking in any fillings that sneak out. Cook 2 to 3 minutes or until golden underneath. Flip and cook 1 to 2 minutes more. Remove from skillet, cut in half, and serve.

Meaty Macaroni

| **<15** | **4 to 6** |
| minutes | servings |

This simple, filling dinner can feed one or the whole family. Plus it freezes well, providing a supply of fast midweek meals.

½ pound noodles, such as ditalini
1½ pounds ground beef
About 1 tablespoon canola oil
Dash of garlic salt
1 jar of your favorite tomato sauce

1. Bring a medium pot of water to a boil. Add noodles and cook 7 to 9 minutes. Drain.

2. While pasta cooks, brown beef in canola oil in a large saucepan. Season with garlic salt. Drain excess fat.

3. Add noodles and tomato sauce, stirring well. Cook on low heat 1 hour, stirring frequently.

Camping Grub

After trekking through wild terrain, setting up camp, and wrasslin' a bear or two, a man needs a hearty meal.

GORP ("Good-Old Raisins and Peanuts") Mix: Combine equal amounts salted peanuts, raisins, and semisweet chocolate chips. For variety, try mixed nuts; dried fruit, such as apricots and bananas; rolled oats; pumpkin or sunflower seeds; or M&M's.

BYO Oatmeal: Fill a small plastic bag with ¼ cup quick-cooking oats, ¼ cup powdered milk, ⅓ cup mixed nuts and diced dried fruit, 1 to 2 teaspoons sugar, and a pinch of cinnamon. When ready to eat, boil in a pot with 1 cup water 2 to 3 minutes.

Make-Ahead Shish Kebabs: In a large plastic bag combine 1½ pounds cubed chicken or beef and chopped vegetables such as mushrooms, peppers, onions, and zucchini. Add your favorite meat marinade (page 59), salad dressing, or BBQ sauce. Marinate in the fridge at least 4 hours or overnight. Discard used marinade (bring extra for brushing). While the grill is heating up, thread skewers, alternating meat and vegetables. Cook about

30 minutes, depending on the heat, rotating several times and brushing with extra marinade.

Sausage and Pepper Sandwiches: Fill each of 4 aluminum-foil packets (page 51) with 4 to 6 ounces sliced sausage. Add ½ cup sliced bell peppers and ¼ cup sliced onions. Seal. Cook over fire 20 to 25 minutes, flipping several times. Remove from heat and cool before opening. Be careful of escaping heat. Just before you're ready to eat, toast 4 hoagie rolls over the fire.

Foil-Pack Beef Stew: Fill each of 4 aluminum-foil packets (page 51) with 4 to 6 ounces cubed beef. Add chopped fresh vegetables, a pat of butter, and some salt and pepper. Seal. Cook over fire 25 to 35 minutes, flipping several times. Cool a few minutes before opening. Be careful of escaping heat.

Campfire S'Mores: Roast a marshmallow over the fire. Place a piece of chocolate bar on a graham cracker. Top with hot roasted marshmallow and another graham cracker. Eat, and then make s'more.

How to Make a Foil Packet

It's easy to make foil packets and fill them with food for grilling ahead of time, so they're ready to throw on the grill or campfire whenever you're ready to eat.

1. Overlap several pieces of heavy-duty aluminum foil (which holds up better to fire and tongs) to create a pouch large enough to hold ingredients.

2. Fold seams tightly all around the food, making sure there are no leaks before placing it in the cooler.

3. When you're ready to cook, place directly on the grill or fire. Flip often using tongs. Beware of escaping steam when opening packets.

Chapter 3

Meat & Potato Dinners

Classic Steak

<30	1
minutes	*serving*

Julia Child said it best: "The only time to eat diet food is while you're waiting for the steak to cook."

1- to 1½-inch-thick marbled steak, such as rib eye,
    strip, or T-bone
Olive oil
Salt and black pepper, or Dry Rub (page 61)

1. Allow steak to come to room temperature. Rub steak all over with olive oil and season with salt and black pepper or dry rub (if using). Wash your hands. Preheat grill to high, and brush rack with more olive oil.

2. Place steak over heat and grill 5 to 6 minutes. Flip using tongs. (Forks can puncture meat, releasing juices. This is bad.) Cook another 5 to 6 minutes for medium. Cook longer for well-done meat or less for rare meat.

3. Do the finger test for doneness: Press steak with your fingertip. Rare should feel soft and spongy; medium should feel moderately soft; well-done should feel firm.

Transfer steak to a plate. Cover with aluminum foil and let rest 5 minutes to seal in juices. Dig in.

Panfried Steak: The best steaks for panfrying are (maximum 1-inch-thick) New York strip, round, sirloin, and tenderloin (aka filet mignon). Once meat comes to room temperature, season all over with salt and pepper or dry rub; wash your hands. In a very hot, heavy-bottomed skillet (or, if you've got one, a cast-iron skillet), panfry steak in a little canola oil 3 to 4 minutes. Flip steak, add 1 pat butter to pan, and cook 3 to 4 minutes more for medium (longer for well-done, less for rarer). Do the finger test for doneness. Cover with aluminum foil, and let rest 5 minutes before digging in.

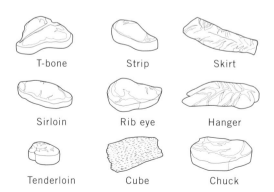

T-bone   Strip   Skirt

Sirloin   Rib eye   Hanger

Tenderloin   Cube   Chuck

Steak Temperature

If you want to use a meat thermometer instead of the finger test for doneness, refer to the chart below.

Type	Internal Temperature*
Rare	125°F to 130°F
Medium-rare	135°F to 140°F
Medium	145°F to 150°F
Medium-well	155°F to 160°F
Well-done	More than 160°F

* **Note:** For maximum safety, an internal temperature of 145°F is recommended.

Jambalaya

60 to 70	6 to 8
minutes	*servings*

When you need a gut-filling recipe, nothing beats this hearty Cajun jambalaya. Serve it steaming hot in big bowls, with hot sauce on the side.

4 teaspoons olive oil

1½ pounds andouille, kielbasa, or other smoked sausage, cut into thick slices

3 pounds boneless, skinless chicken thighs, cut into thick pieces

1 large yellow onion, diced

3 garlic cloves, minced

1 large green bell pepper, diced

4 celery stalks, sliced

1 tablespoon Cajun or Creole seasoning

1 tablespoon Worcestershire sauce

2 cups white rice, uncooked

5 cups chicken broth

1 (28-ounce) can diced tomatoes, with juices

1 pound large shrimp, peeled and deveined

¼ cup flat-leaf parsley, chopped

Salt and black pepper to taste

1. In a deep pot over medium-high heat, warm olive oil. Add sausage and cook until browned, about 5 minutes. Transfer to a bowl.

2. Add chicken to same pot and cook until browned, about 7 minutes. Transfer to the bowl with the sausage. Add onion, garlic, green pepper, and celery. Cook until just tender, about 5 to 7 minutes, stirring a couple times.

3. Return sausage and chicken to pot. Add seasoning, Worcestershire sauce, rice, broth, and tomatoes and stir well. Bring to a boil. Reduce heat, cover, and simmer until rice is fully cooked and has absorbed most of the liquid, about 20 minutes.

4. Stir in shrimp and cook until bright red and opaque, about 5 to 7 minutes. Stir in parsley, and season with salt and pepper.

Meat Marinades

5 minutes	Teriyaki	Fresh Herb	Cajun
	1½ cups	¾ cup	⅔ cup

Like Dry Rubs (page 61), marinades tenderize meat, making it succulent and moist. They come in many varieties, everything from red wine and tequila to soy sauce and cola. A marinade needs two things: an acid, such as beer, cola, lemon juice, vinegar, or wine, and an emulsifier (a fancy word for "fattener"), such as canola, olive, or sesame oil. So get in the kitchen and start experimenting! Here are three simple recipes to get you going.

Teriyaki Marinade: These teriyaki flavors complement chicken, steak, and shrimp. Combine ⅓ cup soy sauce, 1 cup pineapple juice, 2 tablespoons sesame or canola oil, 1 tablespoon Worcestershire sauce, 3 chopped garlic cloves, ¼ teaspoon cayenne pepper, and either ½ teaspoon dried ginger or a 1-inch piece fresh ginger, chopped.

Fresh Herb Marinade: Chicken, fish fillets, lamb, pork, and steak all taste great with a simple herb marinade. Combine ½ cup olive oil, ¼ cup lemon juice, ¼ cup finely chopped herbs (such as basil, cilantro, oregano, and thyme), 4 fresh rosemary sprigs, 2 chopped garlic cloves, and 1 teaspoon each salt and black pepper.

Cajun Marinade: Spicy Cajun flavors add heat to chicken, beef, pork, and ribs. Combine ⅓ cup canola oil, ¼ cup white or apple-cider vinegar, 2 teaspoons garlic powder, 2 teaspoons minced onions, 1 to 2 tablespoons Cajun seasoning, and 1 to 2 tablespoons hot sauce.

For all marinades: Mix ingredients in a bowl. Pour into a large zip-top plastic bag containing meat and refrigerate at least 4 hours, preferably overnight. Let meat rest on countertop 10 minutes before cooking. Remove from plastic bag, discard marinade, and get cooking.

Dry Rub for Meat

5	¾
minutes	*cup*

A dry rub is a simple way to make meat jucier and more flavorful. Get started with this all-purpose mixture, which works well with all types of meat.

    4 tablespoons salt
    2 tablespoons garlic powder
    2 tablespoons onion powder
    2 tablespoons chili powder
    2 tablespoons paprika

1. Combine ingredients in a small bowl; mix well.

2. Using your hands, rub desired amount all over meat before cooking.

Graduate to more complex and flavorful rubs by experimenting with ingredients and adjusting the levels of spiciness, saltiness, and sweetness. Play around with ingredients such as brown sugar, chipotle powder, coriander, cumin, dry mustard, dried sage, and dried thyme to find your favorite combination.

Turkey Carving

Carving a turkey isn't just about looking good while wielding a carving knife. Proper carving enhances meat's juiciness and tenderness. Removing the breast in one piece and slicing it across the grain ensures that each slice contains both well-cooked meat close to the skin and more tender meat close to the bone.

1. When the turkey has finished cooking, move it to a large, clean cutting board and let rest 15 to 20 minutes before carving. Then, grab the end of a drumstick and slide your carving knife into the area between the drumstick and the body. Cut through the joint, not the bone, and pull back on the drumstick until it releases from the body **(a)**.

2. Hold the drumstick by the bony end. Stand it upright at a slight angle to the board and slice the meat into equal-size pieces **(b)**. With a large fork, hold the thigh meat against the cutting board and slice parallel to the bone **(c)**. Arrange all dark meat together on the platter. Remove wings by running your knife along the joint while pulling on the wing with your other hand until it releases **(d)**. Place on a platter.

3. To carve the breasts, slice along the breastbone down the center of the turkey while pulling the meat away from the bone with your other hand **(e)**. Remove the breast in one piece and place on the board. Repeat with other side. Cut the breast meat across the grain **(f)**. Arrange all white meat together on the platter.

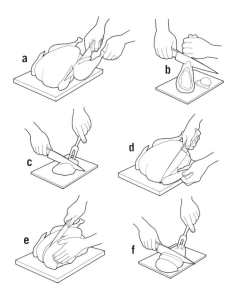

Mashed Potatoes

30	4
minutes	*servings*

M ashed potatoes rule #1: Never, ever buy boxed mashed potatoes. Real men peel potatoes. They also toss in additions like cheese and fresh herbs. Use either Yukon Gold or Red Bliss varieties, which are more flavorful and tender than Russets. Sure, mashed potatoes are perfect with steak, but they're also great with chicken nuggets, pan-fried pork chops, and bacon-wrapped meatloaf.

2½ to 3 pounds potatoes, preferably Yukon Gold,
 peeled and diced
¼ cup butter
¼ cup milk or half-and-half
Generous amounts of salt and black pepper

1. Place potatoes in a large pan and cover with cold water. Bring to a boil. Reduce heat, cover, and cook 12 to 15 minutes, or until tender. Drain.

2. Transfer potatoes to a large bowl. Add remaining ingredients and puree in a food processor or beat with an electric mixer.

Bacon Mashed Potatoes and More

Gussy up your simple spuds by adding any of the following ingredients.

- ½ to ¾ cup diced cooked bacon or pancetta
- ½ to ¾ cup grated Parmesan, cheddar, or goat cheese
- ¼ cup chopped fresh herbs
- 2 tablespoons sour cream
- Some chives
- Bacon pieces
- ½ to ¾ cup caramelized onions or shallots

Pork Chops

<15	4	2 to 4
minutes	chops	servings

W ant dinner on the table in less than 15 minutes? Gentlemen, meet perfect panfried pork chops. Note that boneless and thinner pork chops cook more quickly than bone-in or thicker chops.

1 tablespoon olive oil
4 ½- to ¾-inch-thick boneless pork chops
Salt and black pepper
2 teaspoons Dry Rub (page 61), optional

Warm oil in a large skillet over medium-high heat. Season both sides of chops with salt, pepper, and dry rub (if using). Cook chops 3 minutes. Flip and cook 2 to 3 minutes more, until seared evenly and no pink juices are visible. Remove pan from heat and let chops rest 1 to 2 minutes. Eat.

Sweet-Potato Fries

15	30	4
minutes for prep	*minutes in the oven*	*servings*

Oven-baked sweet-potato fries are tasty and filling. Serve them with burgers, sandwiches, and steaks or just make a big batch, douse them with hot sauce, and wash them down with a cold beer.

2 large sweet potatoes, peeled
2 tablespoons canola or olive oil
Salt and pepper to taste

1. Preheat oven to 400°F. Line a large rimmed baking sheet with aluminum foil. Cut potatoes in half lengthwise, then into wedges or strips. Place in a big bowl. Toss with oil, salt, and pepper.

2. Arrange potatoes in a single layer on the baking sheet. Cook 25 to 30 minutes, turning once or twice, until browned and crispy. Serve with hot sauce, ketchup, and mayonnaise for dipping.

Spicy Sweet-Potato Fries: Toss potatoes with 1 to 2 tablespoons taco seasoning before cooking.

Parmesan-and-Herb Sweet Potato Fries: When nearly finished cooking, remove potatoes from oven. Drizzle with 1 to 2 tablespoons olive oil, ½ cup grated Parmesan, ½ teaspoon red pepper flakes, and either ¼ cup chopped fresh parsley or 2 to 3 tablespoons chopped fresh rosemary. Cook 5 minutes and serve.

Mac & Cheese

15	40	6
minutes for prep	minutes in the oven	servings

Boxed mac & cheese is child's play. Real men make real mac & cheese, which is flavorful and satisfying. Gruyère cheese is a bold, flavorful variety that's available at most major supermarkets. If you prefer a milder flavor, use all sharp white cheddar, all Swiss, or half white and half orange cheddar.

    1 pound elbow macaroni
    ½ cup butter
    ½ cup all-purpose flour
    4½ cups milk
    2 cups sharp white cheddar cheese, divided
    2 cups Gruyère cheese, divided
    Generous amounts of salt and black pepper

1. Preheat oven to 350°F. Grease a deep 2½-quart baking dish with butter or cooking spray.

2. Cook pasta until al dente; drain and set aside.

3. Melt butter in a medium saucepan over medium heat. Whisk in flour. Slowly add milk, whisking continuously, until it reaches a boil. Reduce heat and cook 3 to 5 minutes, stirring constantly. Add 1½ cups cheddar, 1½ cups Gruyère, salt, and pepper. Whisk until smooth; remove from heat. Add cooked pasta to cheese sauce and toss well. Pour into prepared baking dish and top with remaining ½ cup cheddar and ½ cup Gruyère.

4. Bake until cheese bubbles around edges and top turns golden brown, about 35 to 40 minutes.

Tex-Mex Mac & Cheese: Add 2 tablespoons fajita or taco seasoning to cheese sauce.

Italian Mac & Cheese: Substitute mozzarella and Parmesan for the cheddar and Gruyère cheeses and add ¾ to 1 cup cooked diced pancetta or bacon.

Garlicky Spinach

| <10 | 2 |
| *minutes* | *servings* |

Always have a bag of fresh spinach in the fridge, 'cause this recipe is ridiculously easy and flavorful.

1 tablespoon olive oil
1 garlic clove, minced
1 (12- to 14-ounce) bag fresh spinach
A couple pinches crushed red pepper flakes
Several shakes of salt

Heat oil in a large skillet over medium heat. Cook garlic 1 minute. Add spinach. Toss until wilted, about 1 minute. (The spinach will shrink A LOT.) Season with red pepper flakes and salt.

Baked Potato

5	45 to 60	1
minutes for prep	minutes in the oven	serving

A baked potato topped with butter and fresh herbs makes a simple side dish. But with the right combination of hearty toppings, it becomes a satisfying, inexpensive meal. Prepare your favorite toppings, or just look in your fridge for inspiration; leftovers make perfect pile-ons.

  1 Russet potato
  Canola or olive oil, optional
  Toppings of your choice (see suggestions, opposite)

Preheat oven to 350°F. Wash potato, wipe dry, and lightly poke skin all over with a fork (so potato doesn't explode in the oven). Brush with a little oil if you prefer a soft potato skin. Bake on oven rack 45 to 60 minutes, turning occasionally. Cut potato in half lengthwise, being careful of escaping steam. Serve with your favorite toppings.

Baked Potato Toppings

- Butter and salt and pepper or a shake of paprika
- Sour cream and chopped fresh chives
- Bacon Guacamole (page 109)
- Cheddar cheese and crumbled crispy bacon
- Steamed broccoli and cheddar cheese
- Leftover taco filling, cheddar cheese, and salsa
- Beef-and-Beer Chili (page 107)
- Black beans, salsa, and cheddar cheese

Perfect Pasta

10 to 15	9 to 11	5
minutes for prep	minutes for dried pasta	minutes for fresh pasta

The recommended serving size of uncooked pasta is 2 ounces. Most men eat at least 4 ounces.

Pasta scores major points for convenience, afford-ability, ease of preparation, and endless variation. With the following tips, you'll be set for any occasion, from easy weeknight meals like Pasta Carbonara (page 88) to romantic homemade dinners like creamy Shrimp Fettucine (page 86).

1. Use a big pot and fill it about two-thirds high with water. This lets the pasta move around and prevents it from sticking together.

2. Add several pinches of salt to the water, but no oil.*

3. Wait until the water boils, then add the pasta. Cook according to package instructions, stirring occasionally,

---

* **Note:** It's a myth that oil prevents pasta from sticking. You don't need it.

but check the pasta before the end of the recommended cooking time. It should be al dente ("to the tooth"), meaning still firm yet cooked through. Remember that fresh pasta cooks much more quickly than dried.

4. Drain pasta in a colander, but don't rinse it off. Either put it in a big bowl or inside a pot on the stovetop to mix with your sauce.

Ten-Minute Tomato Sauce

10	**3** to **4**
minutes	*servings*

This light tomato sauce couldn't be easier.

1 tablespoon olive oil
1 small shallot, diced
½ garlic clove, minced
1 (28-ounce) can crushed tomatoes
¼ teaspoon crushed red pepper flakes
Several shakes of salt
3 to 4 large basil leaves, thinly sliced

Warm oil in a large pot over medium-high heat. Add shallots and garlic and sauté 2 minutes. Add tomatoes, red pepper flakes, and salt. Bring to a boil. Reduce heat and simmer 7 to 8 minutes, until slightly thickened. Remove from heat and add basil. Serve with your favorite pasta.

Roasted Asparagus

20	4 to 6
minutes	servings

Make friends with asparagus. It's available year-round, it's versatile, and it's delicious. Roasted asparagus tastes great with chicken cutlets, pan-fried pork chops, grilled steak, and baked fish.

2 bunches (about 40 stalks) asparagus,
    bottoms trimmed
2 teaspoons extra-virgin olive oil
Salt to taste
7 to 8 grinds freshly ground black pepper

1. Preheat oven to 400°F. Line a large baking sheet with aluminum foil. Lay asparagus stalks in a straight line across middle of baking sheet. Drizzle with olive oil and season with salt and pepper. Using your hands, gently turn asparagus to coat with oil. Roast 12 to 15 minutes, or until just tender.

Citrus-Spiked Asparagus: Roast asparagus as directed above. In a small bowl, mix the juice of half a lemon, ¼ cup orange juice, 2 teaspoons honey, ¼ teaspoon each orange and lemon zest, salt, and freshly ground black pepper. Heat in a saucepan and drizzle over roasted asparagus.

Roasted Asparagus with Bread Crumbs and Parmesan: Top roasted asparagus with 3 tablespoons plain bread crumbs and ¼ cup grated Parmesan cheese. Bake another 1 to 2 minutes, just until golden brown. Serve immediately.

Spaghetti and Meatballs, Sunday-Gravy Style

2 to **3**
hours

6 to **8**
servings, plus leftover
meatballs and gravy

"Hey, come over here, kid, learn something. . . . You see, you start out with a little bit of oil. Then you fry some garlic. Then you throw in some tomatoes, tomato paste, you fry it; ya make sure it doesn't stick. You get it to a boil; you shove in all your sausage and your meatballs, heh? . . . And a little bit o' wine. An' a little bit o' sugar, and that's my trick."

—*From* The Godfather

One of the best scenes from *The Godfather* is when Clemenza teaches Michael to make the gravy: a rich, red, wine-spiked tomato sauce with lots of meat. So next time you want to feel like a wise guy, make some meatballs and gravy. Whatever you do, just don't call it "sauce."

Gravy

2 tablespoons olive oil, divided
4 sweet Italian sausage links*
2 whole garlic cloves
1 large yellow onion, minced
3 (28-ounce) cans crushed tomatoes
¾ cup red wine
1 teaspoon crushed red pepper flakes
Several shakes of salt

1. In a large, heavy pot over medium-low heat, warm 1 tablespoon olive oil; add sausage. Cook 4 to 5 minutes on each side, or until browned all over. Remove from heat and slice into ¼-inch rounds.

2. Heat remaining tablespoon olive oil in a deep, heavy pot over medium heat. Add garlic and sauté 2 minutes, or until golden and aromatic. Remove garlic and discard. Add onion and cook 3 to 5 minutes. Add tomatoes, red wine, red pepper flakes, and salt. Bring to a boil, then lower heat and simmer about 1 hour, stirring occasionally until deep red in color.

---

* **Note:** Sweet Italian sausage is available at Italian specialty markets, delis, and most major supermarkets.

Meatballs

Makes about 2 dozen meatballs

½ pound ground beef

½ pound ground pork

1 cup plain bread crumbs (or more as needed)

⅓ cup grated Parmigiano Reggiano cheese

¼ cup fresh flat-leaf parsley, chopped

1 egg, lightly beaten (or more as needed)

A few pinches each salt and black pepper

2 tablespoons olive oil

2 tablespoons canola oil

1 pound spaghetti

½ cup grated Parmigiano Reggiano cheese

8 to 10 large fresh basil leaves, thinly sliced

More Parmigiano Reggiano and basil for serving

1. Place meats in a large bowl. Add bread crumbs, cheese, parsley, egg, salt, and pepper. Mix with your hands until everything is moistened and meat holds together. If it's too dry, add a bit of water or another beaten egg. If it's too moist, add more bread crumbs. Once the consistency is right, roll into 1½-inch balls.

2. Warm oils in a large skillet over medium heat. Fit as many meatballs in skillet as you can without overcrowding.

Cook 2 to 3 minutes until browned, then turn over and cook another 2 to 3 minutes; continue cooking and turning until all sides are evenly browned. Transfer cooked meatballs to a paper-towel-lined plate to absorb excess oil. Repeat until all meatballs are cooked.

4. Add cooked meatballs and sausage to gravy. Simmer an additional 60 minutes (or up to 3 hours for a thicker, richer sauce). If sauce becomes too thick, thin with a little water or water mixed with a bit of red wine. Stir in basil just before serving. Scoop out a few meatballs and sausage pieces for presentation.

5. While gravy simmers, cook pasta in salted water until al dente, drain, and place in a large serving dish. Add gravy, top with the reserved meatballs and sausage, and sprinkle with more Parmigiano Reggiano and basil.

Baked Meatballs: You can bake meatballs instead of frying them in step 2. Preheat oven to 400°F. Place meatballs on a foil-lined baking sheet and bake 20 minutes, or until browned.

Fish

Panfried	Baked	4
<20 minutes	25 minutes	4- to 6-ounce fillets

Whether you catch it in the ocean or find in the freezer section of the supermarket, fish is a healthy, quick meal. Panfrying creates a crisp exterior and tender interior; oven-baking makes fish flaky and delicious. As a general rule, cook thin (½-inch-thick) fillets, such as catfish and tilapia, 3 to 4 minutes per side; medium (¾-inch-thick) fillets, such as cod and sea bass, 4 to 5 minutes per side; thick (1-inch or thicker) fillets, such as halibut and swordfish steaks, 6 to 7 minutes per side. Fish should be opaque and browned on the outside. If it isn't, cook a little longer.

Panfried Fish: Heat 1 tablespoon olive oil in a large skillet over medium-high heat. Season both sides of 4 fillets of tilapia (or other white fish) with salt and pepper. Add fish to pan; cook until lightly browned and crisp, about 4 minutes per side. Place fish on a plate and serve with lemon wedges, hot sauce, and tartar sauce.

Baked Fish: In a small bowl, mix 3 tablespoons melted butter, juice of half a lemon, 1 small minced garlic clove, 2 tablespoons chopped fresh flat-leaf parsley, salt, and black pepper. Place 4 (4- to 6-ounce) fillets of tilapia or other white fish (such as catfish, grouper, or snapper) in a large baking dish coated with cooking spray. Pour butter mixture overtop. Bake 20 minutes at 425°F or until golden brown on the outside.

Super-Healthy Fish: Drizzle fish with some olive oil, lemon juice, and salt and pepper. Bake as above. Season with fresh herbs.

Fish Toppings

These simple toppings make a good fish fillet even better.

Piccatta-Style: Mix a few tablespoons melted butter, lemon juice, parsley, capers, salt, and pepper.

Salsa: Top each fillet with a spoonful of pesto or fruity salsa like mango.

California-Style: Diced ripe avocado, lime juice, scallions, and chili powder.

Shrimp Fettuccine

25	2
minutes	*servings*

S he wants a romantic dinner to be simply delicious. You want it to be deliciously simple. Sparks will fly for both of you with lemon and white-wine-spiked creamy noodles and shrimp. Serve with a side salad and white wine, such as Chardonnay or Pinot Grigio.

8 ounces pasta noodles, such as fettuccine
   or tagliatelle
2 to 3 teaspoons butter
1 small garlic clove, minced
½ pound extra-large shrimp (about 15), deveined,
   cleaned, and tails removed
⅓ cup dry white wine
4 canned artichoke hearts, sliced into quarters
Zest of half a lemon
¾ cup heavy cream
Salt and black pepper
⅓ cup grated Parmesan cheese
4 to 5 large, fresh basil leaves, thinly sliced
Grated Parmesan cheese and fresh basil to garnish
   (optional)

1. Cook the pasta in salted water until al dente. Drain, but do not rinse.

2. In a large pan over medium heat, melt butter. Add garlic and sauté 1 minute, until lightly golden. Add shrimp and sauté 2 to 3 minutes, until they turn bright red. Transfer to a plate.

3. Add wine to the same pan. Let simmer 1 to 2 minutes, until wine reduces. Add artichoke hearts, lemon zest, heavy cream, and salt and pepper. Simmer on low heat for 3 to 5 minutes, or until slightly thickened. Do not let it boil or the cream will separate. Return shrimp to the pan and cook about 2 minutes.

4. Add cooked pasta to the pan and toss to coat. Turn off heat, and stir in cheese and basil. Serve hot.

Pasta Carbonara

<15	4
minutes	*servings, or 2 if you're really hungry*

M eat, eggs, and cheese. Pasta doesn't get any manlier than a good carbonara.

1 pound linguine, fettuccini, or thick spaghetti

1 tablespoon olive oil

½ pound pancetta, chopped*

4 eggs

A few dashes salt

½ teaspoon black pepper

⅔ cups grated Parmesan cheese, plus more
   for garnish

1. Cook pasta in salted water according to package instructions until al dente. Meanwhile, in a large skillet over medium heat, warm oil and cook pancetta until lightly brown but still tender, about 5 minutes. Remove from heat.

---

* **Note:** Pancetta (Italian bacon) is available at Italian markets and delis as well as most supermarkets.

2. In a large bowl, whisk together eggs, salt, and black pepper; then whisk in cheese. Drain cooked pasta (reserving a little bit of pasta water). Working quickly (so eggs don't cook), add cooked pasta to skillet with pancetta. Using some muscle, quickly and vigorously stir in egg–cheese mixture. If it seems dry, add a little reserved pasta water. Top with more grated cheese, if you'd like, and eat immediately.

Poor Man's Pasta Carbonara: Substitute bacon for pancetta.

Easy Homemade Pizza

10 to 15	15	1
minutes	minutes	pizza
for prep	in the oven	(4 servings)

Domino's may be in your fave five, but at some point a man has to make his own pizza. It's easier than you might think and doesn't require any special equipment. Whether you roll out the dough or top a store-bought crust, it's still technically homemade.

1 pound pizza dough (if frozen, thaw completely
   before using)
Olive oil
½ cup jarred marinara sauce
1 cup shredded mozzarella, divided
Toppings of your choice (page 92)

1. Preheat oven to 475°F. Line a large baking sheet with parchment paper or coat with cooking spray or olive oil.

2. Place dough on a lightly floured surface and roll out into a rectangle. Transfer to baking sheet and brush top with a little olive oil. Spread marinara sauce overtop, leaving

a ½-inch border. Sprinkle with half the mozzarella. Add toppings and remaining mozzarella.

3. Bake 15 minutes, or until cheese is melted and bottom of crust is brown. Eat it while it's hot.

Pizza Toppings

- Pepperoni and cheese
- Pepperoni, sausage, salami, green bell peppers, and onions
- Sliced steak (page 54), mushrooms, onions, and provolone
- Sausage, green bell peppers, and onions
- Italian sausage, pepperoncini, and provolone
- Prosciutto, onions, and basil
- Meatballs and mushrooms
- Ground beef, black beans, salsa, scallions, and cheddar
- Canadian bacon and pineapple chunks
- Chicken, BBQ sauce, and cheddar
- Chicken and pesto
- *Quattro Formaggio* ("four cheese")—Asiago, Gorgonzola, mozzarella, pecorino Romano— and basil
- Eggplant, roasted red peppers, spinach, and tomatoes
- Green bell peppers, mushrooms, olives, and onions
- Red onions, tomatoes, artichoke hearts, olives, and feta

Potato Wedges

<15	45 to 60	4
minutes for prep	minutes in the oven	servings

M aster making roasted potato wedges, since they'll round out any dinner. And use Red Bliss or Yukon Gold potatoes for an extra crunchy exterior and tender interior.

2 pounds small potatoes, washed, dried, and quartered

3 tablespoons olive oil

1 teaspoon salt

½ teaspoon black pepper

2 to 3 tablespoons chopped fresh rosemary, optional

Preheat oven to 400°F. Place potatoes in a big bowl. Drizzle with oil; season with salt, pepper, and rosemary (if using). Stir well. Place potatoes in a large baking dish or rimmed baking sheet. Roast 45 to 60 minutes, stirring halfway through cooking, until browned and crispy.

Beef Stew

25 *minutes* *for prep*	**1½** *hours* *cooking time*	**6** to **8** *servings*

N othing tastes better on a freezing winter day than a piping hot bowl of beef stew.

3 tablespoons olive oil

2 pounds top-round or chuck steak, cut into
    ½-inch cubes

¼ cup all-purpose flour, seasoned with a little salt
    and pepper

1 large yellow onion, diced

1½ cups red wine

3 cups beef broth, plus more as needed

1½ pounds potatoes, peeled and cut into ½-inch cubes

3 carrots, peeled and sliced

½ cup flat-leaf parsley, chopped plus extra
    for garnish

2 teaspoons fresh thyme or 1 teaspoon dried thyme

Salt and black pepper to taste

1. Heat olive oil in a large, deep pot. Dredge meat in seasoned flour. Place in hot oil and cook until browned, about 5 minutes. (Don't overcrowd meat or it'll steam.) Transfer browned meat to a bowl.

2. In same pot, add diced onion and brown 3 to 5 minutes. Deglaze pot with wine: Pour wine into pot and use a wooden spoon to scrape brown bits from the bottom. Add cooked meat to the pot. Cover and cook over low heat 25 to 30 minutes.

3. Add broth, potatoes, and carrots. Cover and cook over low heat until meat is very tender, about 1 hour, stirring occasionally. Add more broth if you prefer a soupier stew. When meat is cooked, stir in herbs, salt, and pepper. Top each serving with a couple pinches of parsley and serve.

Chapter 4

Beer, Bacon & Bar Food

Greens with Bacon

| 15 minutes | 2 to 3 servings |

Salty, smoky bacon balances the bitterness of greens, making them go down much more easily. For extra-soft greens, follow recipe as below. Then add ¼ to ⅓ cup chicken broth, white wine, or beer (seriously) and cook, partially covered, another 15 to 20 minutes.

"Life expectancy would grow by leaps and bounds if green vegetables smelled as good as bacon."

—*Doug Larson*

3 slices bacon

1 yellow onion, diced

1 bunch greens, such as Swiss chard, kale, mustard greens, or collards (though collards need to cook a little longer), rinsed, stems removed, and chopped

Salt and freshly ground black pepper to taste

1. In a large skillet over medium-high heat, cook bacon 2 to 3 minutes, until it gives up some fat (making skillet greasy) but is still soft. Remove bacon and drain on a paper-towel-lined plate.

2. Add onion to skillet with bacon fat and cook 3 minutes. Add chopped greens and cook, tossing a few times, until wilted, about 5 minutes. Season generously with salt and black pepper. Serve.

Lobster with Beer and Butter Sauce

25	3
minutes	*servings*

E very man should know how to kill a giant bug in the kitchen, whether it's a daddy longlegs crawling on the windowsill or a couple of lobsters chilling in the fridge. Keep these scrumptuous crustaceans cold on ice until dinnertime. Then use this simple recipe to infuse succulent lobster meat with beer and seasonings.

1 (12-ounce) bottle beer
1 tablespoon salt
2 tablespoons Old Bay seasoning
⅛ teaspoon pepper
2 to 3 (1- to 2- pound) lobsters
Butter or butter sauce

1. In a large, deep pot over medium-high heat, combine 3 quarts water with beer, Old Bay, and pepper. Bring it to a boil.

2. Use a dish towel or oven mitt to hold a lobster by its back, claws pointed away from you and any bystanders. Clip off rubber bands and drop lobster into boiling water. Don't be alarmed if the tail twitches while it boils; it's just a reflex reaction to the heat. Repeat for additional lobsters. Cook 7 to 9 minutes, or until shells are dark red.

3. Remove with tongs. Use a sharp chef's knife to cut down the back and through the claws. Serve with lemons and butter or butter sauce on the side.

Browned Beer-Infused Lobster: After boiling 5 minutes in step 2, use tongs to remove cooked lobster to a cutting board. Use a sharp knife to cut a rectangle out of the top of the shell, brush butter over the meat, and place the lobster under a broiler for 3 minutes, until top is browned.

Butter Sauce: In a saucepan over medium heat, melt about 3 tablespoons butter. Gradually stir in 3 tablespoons flour, ½ teaspoon salt, ⅛ teaspoon pepper, and 1½ cups hot water. Boil 5 minutes; add 3 more tablespoons butter and stir until smooth and creamy.

Happy Lobsters: If your date is squeamish, hypnotize lobsters before placing them in the boiling water by rubbing the top of their heads or abdomens. The theory behind lobster hypnotism is that the adrenaline produced by a frightened lobster negatively affects the texture and flavor of the meat, and pacifying them first makes the eating experience more enjoyable. Sounds silly, but perhaps it'll tenderize your lobsters and warm your date's heart at the same time.

Bacon-Wrapped Meatloaf

15	1	4 to 6
minutes for prep	*hour in the oven*	*servings*

M eatloaf tastes even better the next day, so plan on making some delicious sandwiches for lunch. If you (or those you are feeding) are a die-hard bacon enthusiast, serve this alongside Bacon Mashed Potatoes (page 65).

1 tablespoon canola oil

1 small yellow onion, diced

2 pounds ground beef (85% lean is best)

¾ cup plain bread crumbs

2 eggs, lightly beaten

1 tablespoon Worcestershire sauce

2 tablespoons spicy mustard

1 teaspoon salt

1 teaspoon black pepper

Several dashes hot sauce

6 tablespoons ketchup, divided

8 to 10 slices bacon

1. Preheat oven to 350°F. Heat oil in a large skillet over medium-high heat. Add onions and sauté 3 to 5 minutes, or until lightly browned; let cool slightly.

2. In a large bowl, combine sautéed onions with all ingredients from ground beef through hot sauce, plus 2 tablespoons ketchup. Using your hands, mix until thoroughly combined. Transfer beef mixture onto a large baking sheet lightly greased with canola oil or cooking spray. Shape into an oval mound and lay bacon slices over the top so that they crisscross. Wash your hands, then brush remaining 4 tablespoons ketchup over bacon and meatloaf.

3. Bake 50 to 60 minutes, or until browned on top and cooked through. (A thermometer inserted into the thickest part of the meatloaf should read 160 to 165°F. If you don't have a thermometer, insert a knife into the thickest part to ensure meat is no longer pink).

Beer Bread

| <10 minutes for prep | 40 to 45 minutes in the oven | 6 to 8 servings |

The next time you need something tasty to sop up the juices of your beef stew or chili, make a loaf of this flavorful bread.

3 cups all-purpose flour
1 tablespoon baking powder
1 teaspoon salt
3 tablespoons sugar
1 (12-ounce) bottle beer, preferably dark, such as porter or stout

1. Preheat oven to 400°F. Coat an 8-by-4-inch or 9-by-5-inch loaf pan with cooking spray.

2. In a large bowl, stir together all ingredients. Pour into pan. Bake 40 to 45 minutes, or until top is golden brown and a toothpick inserted into the center comes out clean. Cool on a rack 10 minutes before removing from pan. Cool completely.

Cheddar Beer Bread: Stir 1 cup grated sharp cheddar cheese into batter.

Cheddar-Dill Beer Bread: Stir 1 cup grated sharp cheddar cheese and ½ cup chopped fresh dill (or 1 to 2 tablespoons dried dill) into batter.

Beef-and-Beer Chili

30 to 45 minutes | **6 to 8** servings

"No soldier can fight properly unless he is properly fed on beef and beer."

—Duke of Marlborough

This no-fuss, quick-cook chili is perfect for game day yet easy enough for a midweek meal. Bonus: It tastes even better the next day.

1 tablespoon canola or olive oil

1 large yellow onion, diced

1 large green or red bell pepper, chopped

1 to 1¼ pound ground beef

1½ to 2 tablespoons chili powder

1 teaspoon cayenne pepper

1 teaspoon ground cumin

Several shakes of salt

2 tablespoons light brown sugar

2 (14.5-ounce) cans pinto or red kidney beans, drained

1 (14.5-ounce) can diced tomatoes, with juices

1 (12-ounce) bottle dark beer, such as stout

1 tablespoon cornmeal, optional

1. Warm oil in a large pot over medium-high heat. Add onions and peppers and sauté 5 minutes. Add meat. Cook until browned, about 10 minutes. Stir in spices, salt, and brown sugar. Add beans, tomatoes, and beer. Stir and bring to a boil. Reduce heat to low and simmer 20 to 25 minutes, or until thick and soupy. Stir in cornmeal if you want a thicker chili.

2. Serve chili hot, topped with any of the following: shredded cheddar cheese, sour cream, diced avocado, sliced scallions, or fresh cilantro.

Bacon Guacamole

15	**6 to 8**
minutes	*servings*

Scooped up with nachos or rolled into Breakfast Burritos (page 32), guacamole is good on its own. But bacon guacamole is truly awesome.

6 slices bacon

Flesh of 2 ripe avocados

1 medium tomato, chopped

4 scallions (white parts only), finely chopped

Juice of 1 lime

A couple pinches salt

A couple dashes hot sauce

Small handful fresh cilantro leaves, finely chopped

1. Place bacon in a skillet over medium-high heat and cook until crisp. Drain on a paper-towel-lined plate. Let cool and chop into small pieces.

2. Combine remaining ingredients in a blender or food processor and pulse until chunky.

Beer-Battered Onion Rings

45	4 to 6
minutes	*servings*

These onion rings are irresistibly thick and crunchy. Plus they're made with beer.

1¾ cups all-purpose flour
1 teaspoon seasoned salt, such as Lawry's
1 teaspoon baking powder
½ teaspoon black pepper
1 (12-ounce) bottle beer, preferably dark
2 large sweet onions, such as Bermuda, Vidalia, or Walla Walla, sliced into ½-inch-thick rounds and separated into rings
Canola oil for frying

1. In a medium bowl, combine flour, seasoned salt, baking powder, and pepper. Slowly add beer. Set aside.

2. Place onion rings in a bowl of ice water and let chill 15 minutes. Remove onion from water and pat dry with paper towels. Fill a medium heavy-bottomed pot with 2 inches of canola oil and heat to 370°F. (It's ready when a little batter dropped into the oil bubbles and

floats immediately to the top.) Dip each onion ring in batter, letting excess drip into bowl.

3. Fry onion rings in batches, being careful not to over-crowd. Cook 1 to 2 minutes per side or until golden brown. If they're too dark, lower the heat. Transfer to a paper-towel-lined plate to drain. Serve with ketch-up, ranch dressing, Thousand Island dressing, spicy mustard, BBQ sauce, or any condiment you like.

Beer Margarita

5	6 to 8
minutes	*servings*

"Beer is proof that God loves us and wants us to be happy."

—*Ben Franklin*

A nd frosty Beer Margaritas make us *really* happy. Agave nectar is available at organic markets and some liquor stores; simple syrup is a good substitute.

1½ cups tequila
½ cup Grand Marnier
⅓ bottle beer
1 can frozen lemonade concentrate
Juice of 1 lime
Juice of half a lemon
½ cup agave nectar (or simple syrup)

Add all ingredients to a blender. Fill with ice and blend until smooth. Serve in margarita or rocks glasses.

Spicy Black Bean Dip

<15	6 to 8
minutes	*servings*

Got a tailgate, potluck, or birthday bash to go to? Offer to bring this zingy dip along with some chips. You'll be the hit of the party.

2 (15-ounce) cans black beans, drained
1 small red onion, diced
1 garlic clove, chopped
1 small jalapeño
1 tablespoon lime juice
1 cup of your favorite salsa
2 tablespoons mayonnaise or sour cream
Small handful fresh cilantro leaves, chopped
1 teaspoon ground cumin, optional
Salt and black pepper to taste

Combine all ingredients in a blender or food processor and pulse until chunky. Transfer to a bowl. Serve with tortilla chips.

Chicken Nuggets

>25 *minutes*   **4** to **6** *servings*

Chicken nuggets are to kids what beer is to guys. So the next time you're cooking for little ones, make these bite-size nibbles and serve them with BBQ sauce, ranch dressing, or tomato sauce.

Canola or peanut oil for frying
2 pounds chicken tenders (cut in half if they're big)
A pinch each salt and black pepper
⅔ cup all-purpose flour
3 large eggs, lightly beaten
1 cup bread crumbs, plain or seasoned

1. In a medium skillet over medium-high heat, heat 1 to 2 inches of oil. Season chicken with salt and pepper. In one shallow dish, place flour. In a second dish, add egg. In a third dish, add bread crumbs. Dredge each chicken tender in flour first **(a)**, then egg **(b)**, then bread crumbs **(c)**.

2. Cook breaded chicken **(d)**, a few pieces at a time, 3 to 4 minutes, or until golden brown and crisp. If they're burning, lower the heat. Place on a paper-towel-lined plate to drain.

Baked Nuggets: Arrange chicken pieces on a greased baking sheet for 20 minutes and pop into an oven preheated to 400°F, or until golden and crisp.

Buffalo Wings

>25	4
minutes	*servings*

A great buffalo chicken wing should be fried to crispy-on-the-outside, moist-on-the-inside perfection and taste just spicy enough to make your eyes water. Just in case, keep the hot-sauce bottle on the table.

Canola oil for frying
5 to 6 pounds (about 2 dozen) chicken wings, pointy tips removed and patted dry

Buffalo Sauce:
½ cup melted butter
1 cup vinegar-based hot sauce
2 tablespoons apple cider vinegar

1. Pour 4 to 5 inches canola oil into a medium pot over high heat. When oil is very hot (about 350°F)*, add chicken and cook 10 minutes, or until golden and crisp.

---

* **Note:** To test oil's heat without a thermometer, drop a little batter into it: If oil bubbles and batter floats immediately to the top, it's time to start frying.

Cook in batches to avoid overcrowding. Transfer cooked wings to a paper-towel-lined plate.

2. In a large bowl, whisk together sauce ingredients. Add wings and toss until well coated.

Baked Buffalo Wings: Spread chicken wings in a single layer on a large baking sheet. Drizzle with 1 tablespoon canola oil and season with salt and black pepper. Bake at 425°F, turning once, 25 to 30 minutes, or until golden brown and crispy.

Blue-Cheese Dipping Sauce: Combine 1 cup mayonnaise, 1 cup plain yogurt, and 1 cup crumbled blue cheese in a small bowl. Serve with celery sticks.

Ten-Minute Tortilla Pizza

10	1
minutes	*pizza*

When you're hungry, tired, and too broke to order pizza, make this crispy, cheesy snack. It's a perfect hybrid of nachos and pizza—and it'll be in your belly in ten minutes or less.

 1 (6- or 8-inch) flour tortilla
 1 to 2 tablespoons pizza sauce
 Toppings, such as black beans, green peppers, olives, and cooked sausage
 Your favorite shredded melting cheese

Preheat oven broiler. Place tortillas on a baking sheet coated with cooking spray. Spread sauce, toppings, and cheese overtop. Broil 7 to 8 minutes minutes, or until cheese melts and the edges are crispy.

Real Beer Float

1	1
minute	float

What could make an ice-cream soda even better? The addition of booze, of course. This basic recipe lends itself to endless variations: Try chocolate and coffee ice cream instead of vanilla, or top the float with a swirl of whipped cream and a dash of cocoa powder or chocolate syrup. Or add a splash of liqueur such as amaretto, Bailey's Irish cream, or Grand Marnier.

    1 bottle dark beer, such as porter or stout
    1 big scoop vanilla ice cream

1. Pour beer in a glass.

2. Add ice cream.

3. Drink.

Sweet-and-Salty Snack Mix

10	1	10 to 14
minutes for prep	hour in the oven	servings

It's a well-known fact that men cannot watch sports without eating snacks. So keep this recipe next to the remote, where you know you won't lose it. For a sweeter mix, try substituting honey-roasted peanuts for the salted peanuts. Stored in an airtight container, it'll keep for 3 to 5 days.

2 cups mini pretzels

2 cups crunchy cereal, such as Corn Chex

2 cups cheese crackers, such as Cheez-Its

2 cups oyster crackers or mini wheat crackers

2 cups salted peanuts

½ cup melted butter

4 tablespoons light brown sugar

2 tablespoons Worcestershire sauce

2 tablespoons hot sauce

1. Preheat oven to 250°F. In a large bowl, combine pretzels, cereal, cheese crackers, oyster or mini wheat crackers, and peanuts.

2. In a small bowl, combine melted butter, brown sugar, Worcestershire sauce, and hot sauce; stir well. Pour over snack mix, stirring until well coated.

3. Transfer mixture to 2 large baking sheets covered with aluminum foil. Bake, stirring 3 or 4 times, 1 hour, or until golden and crisp.

Bacon Brownies

30	18
minutes	*brownies*

Just when you thought brownies couldn't get better, along comes these sweet and salty slabs of chocolate goodness, studded with bits of crisp, salty, smoky bacon.

6 bacon strips
1 package store-bought brownie mix
Store-bought caramel sauce, warmed, for serving
Whipped cream for serving

1. Cook bacon in a large skillet over medium-high heat until somewhat crispy. Drain on a paper-towel-lined plate. Chop 4 strips into small pieces, reserving 2 strips for garnish.

2. Make brownie batter according to package directions and stir in chopped bacon; pour into a greased 8-inch-square baking pan. For optimal bacon distribution, swirl a spatula through batter. Bake according to chart on package.

3. To serve, place a brownie on a plate. Drizzle with warm caramel. Place a dollop of whipped cream on top and sprinkle with reserved chopped bacon. Await praise.

Better-Than-Movie Popcorn

| <5 minutes | 10 to 12 servings |

Whether you're relaxing after a long day at work or throwing back a few beers with the guys, freshly popped popcorn can't be beat.

About 3 tablespoons canola oil
About ½ cup corn kernels
Toppings (page 125)

1. In a large saucepan, add enough canola oil to coat bottom. Cover and place over heat high. After 1 or 2 minutes, toss a couple kernels into the pan. If they start whirring and spinning, the oil is ready.

2. Add enough kernels to cover bottom of pan. Cover and give the pan a couple shakes to coat kernels with oil. Now listen for popping. Shake pan a few times as corn pops.

3. Once it really gets going, leave it alone. When the popping slows, remove pan from heat quickly or popcorn will burn. Pour popcorn into a big bowl, add your favorite toppings, and toss.

Popcorn Toppings

Mix up these gooey delicious toppings to take freshly popped corn (page 123) or regular microwaved popcorn to the next level.

Hot-and-Spicy Popcorn: Mix ¼ cup melted butter, several dashes hot sauce, and 1 tablespoon taco seasoning. Pour over popcorn and toss.

Pizza Popcorn: Mix ¼ cup melted butter, 1 tablespoon Italian seasoning, and ½ cup grated Parmesan. Pour over popcorn.

Maple-Nut Popcorn: Bring to a boil 1 cup maple syrup, 3 tablespoons butter, and 1¼ teaspoons salt. Lower heat and cook 3 minutes at a slow bubble until slightly thickened. Remove from heat. Place popcorn and 1 cup nuts of your choice in a large greased bowl. Pour syrup over popcorn and toss well. Transfer to 2 aluminum-foil-lined baking sheets. Bake at 325°F for 10 minutes, or until just golden and toasty. Remove and let cool. Break into clusters.

Chapter 5

Chocolate, Cheesecake & More

Oatmeal Chocolate Chunk Cookies

15 to 20	30 to 40	40
minutes for prep	minutes in the oven	cookies

Nothing says you're a good guy more than baking cookies, especially oatmeal ones. So if you've got some damage control to do, get baking.

3 cups rolled (not quick-cooking) oats

1¼ cups all-purpose flour

½ teaspoon baking soda

1 teaspoon salt

½ teaspoon cinnamon

1 cup (2 sticks) unsalted butter

1 cup white sugar

½ cup light brown sugar

2 eggs

1 tablespoon vanilla extract

1 cup semisweet chocolate chunks (cut from a block of chocolate) or chocolate chips, if you'd like

½ cup sweetened flaked coconut

½ cup coarsely chopped pecans or walnuts

1. Preheat oven to 350°F. Line 2 baking sheets with parchment paper.

2. In a medium bowl, stir together oats, flour, baking soda, salt, and cinnamon.

3. In a large bowl, combine butter and sugars. Using an electric mixer on medium speed, beat until creamy. Add eggs and vanilla, beating until just combined. Beat in dry ingredients. Stir in chocolate, coconut, and nuts.

4. Drop dough, 1 heaping tablespoonful at a time, on baking sheets; place 2 inches apart (they will spread during baking). If baking both sheets at once, place racks in the upper and lower thirds of the oven and switch halfway through baking time. Otherwise, bake one sheet at a time in middle of oven.

5. Bake cookies 18 minutes, or until golden brown. Transfer to a rack to cool. Cool completely before storing and place in an airtight container.

Milkshakes

5	1
minutes	*serving*

Want to feel like a kid again? Make a cold, frothy milkshake. They always make you smile. For a classic finish, top with whipped cream, chocolate sauce, and a maraschino cherry. Here are some favorite flavors.

Vanilla: In a blender, place 1 cup milk, 2 cups vanilla ice cream, and ¼ teaspoon vanilla extract (optional).

Chocolate: In a blender, place 1 cup milk and 2 cups chocolate ice cream *or* 1 cup milk, 2 cups vanilla ice cream, and 3 to 4 tablespoons chocolate syrup.

Mint-Chocolate: In a blender, place 1 cup milk, 2 cups chocolate ice cream, and ¼ teaspoon peppermint extract.

Strawberry: In a blender, place 1 cup milk, 2 cups strawberry or vanilla ice cream, and ½ cup frozen or fresh strawberries.

Banana: In a blender, place 1 cup milk, 2 cups vanilla ice cream, and 1 small banana, sliced. Blend on high about 15 seconds. Add 2 cups vanilla ice cream.

For all flavors: Blend 15 to 20 seconds on low, so the ice cream doesn't melt too much. It should be thick and frothy.

Six Classic Cocktails

These classics won't let you down.

"To alcohol! The cause of—and solution to—all of life's problems."

—Homer Simpson

Old-Fashioned: Muddle 1 maraschino cherry, 1 orange slice, 1 teaspoon sugar, 1 to 2 dashes Angostura bitters, and 1 teaspoon water in a chilled old-fashioned glass. Remove orange rind. Add 2 ounces rye or bourbon whiskey and ice; stir. Garnish with a maraschino cherry and an orange slice.

Manhattan: Stir 2 ounces straight rye or bourbon whiskey, 1 ounce sweet vermouth, and 1 dash Angostura bitters in a pitcher half filled with ice (or shake with ice). Strain into a chilled cocktail glass and garnish with a maraschino cherry.

Cosmopolitan: Combine ¾ ounce vodka, ½ ounce triple sec, 1 ounce cranberry juice, and ½ ounce lime juice with ice in a cocktail shaker. Shake and strain into a chilled martini glass.

Vodka Gimlet: Combine 1½ ounces vodka, 1 ounce lime juice, and 1 teaspoon powdered sugar with ice in a cocktail shaker. Shake and strain into a martini glass.

Martini: Depending on your taste, mix 5 to 8 parts gin with 1 part vermouth for a dry martini. For an even drier martini, use less vermouth. Stir in a pitcher half filled with ice, or shake with ice, and then strain into a chilled cocktail glass. Garnish with green olives or lemon peel. A "bone-dry" martini, also known as "pass the bottle," contains no vermouth whatsoever.

Champagne Cocktail: Add 1 dash Angostura bitters to 1 sugar cube in the bottom of a chilled Champagne glass and slowly pour in cold, dry champagne. Garnish with a twist of lemon peel.

No-Bake Cheesecake

10	6 to 8
minutes	servings

You can't go wrong with a classic cheesecake for dessert. This simple recipe is so creamy and delicious, your friends won't believe it takes only 10 minutes to make.

- 1 (8-ounce) package cream cheese, softened
- 1 cup sour cream
- ½ cup sugar
- 2 teaspoons vanilla extract
- 1 (8-ounce) container nondairy whipped topping
- 1 graham cracker pie crust or Oreo Cookie pie crust

In a large bowl, stir cream cheese, sour cream, sugar, and vanilla extract until smooth. Fold in whipped topping. Pour filling into crust and chill at least 4 hours, or preferably overnight. Add toppings of your choice, cut into slices, and serve.

Variations include:

Chocolate-Raspberry Cheesecake: Top with chocolate sauce and fresh raspberries.

Turtle Cheesecake: Top with caramel sauce, chocolate sauce, and chopped pecans.

Cherry Cheesecake: Top with canned cherry pie filling.

Mint-Chocolate Cheesecake: Add 1 teaspoon peppermint extract to the batter, top with crushed mint-chocolate cookies or candies, and drizzle with chocolate sauce.

Sexy Strawberries Zabaglione

| <15
| *minutes*

There's so much more to after-dinner romance than a can of whipped cream. *Zabaglione* (pronounced "zah-habl-YOH-nay") is a light, elegant dessert that's easy to make yet seriously seductive. It's made with strawberries and wine or Champagne. Plus it's Italian. That's sexy.

8 to 10 fresh strawberries, sliced

2 egg yolks

2 tablespoons sugar

2 tablespoons sweet Marsala wine or Champagne

1. Divide sliced strawberries between two wine or martini glasses. Set aside.

2. In a large metal or glass bowl, combine egg yolks, sugar, and wine or Champagne. Whisk vigorously (or beat with an electric mixer).

3. Place the bowl over a saucepan filled with 1 to 2 inches simmering water, making sure the bottom of the bowl doesn't touch the water **(a)**. Continue to whisk or beat until doubled in volume and thick, about 5 minutes **(b)**.

4. Spoon over berries and serve **(c)**. Be self-deprecating when she "oohs" and "ahhhs."

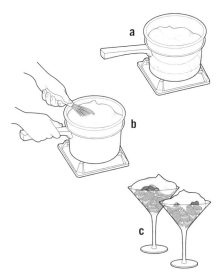

Mom's All-Purpose Chocolate Cake

45 to 65
minutes

1
double-layer
cake

E very man needs a basic chocolate cake recipe that's delicious, super easy to make, and perfect for festive occasions ranging from romantic dinners to birthday parties. With my mom's recipe, I know you're in good hands.

1 cup cocoa powder

2½ cups all-purpose flour

1 teaspoon baking powder

1½ teaspoons baking soda

½ teaspoon salt

2½ sticks (1¼ cup) unsalted butter,
    at room temperature

2 cups sugar

3 eggs, at room temperature

1 cup sour cream

2 teaspoons vanilla extract

1. Place a rack in the middle of the oven and preheat to 350°F. Grease 2 9-inch-round cake pans with cooking spray or butter.

2. In a small bowl, whisk 1 cup hot water with cocoa powder until smooth; set aside. In a medium bowl, combine flour, baking powder, baking soda, and salt; set aside. In a large bowl, beat butter and sugar with an electric mixer on medium-high speed until light and fluffy, about 3 minutes. Mix in eggs and sour cream.

3. Add flour mixture to butter mixture in three additions (this is so that the flour doesn't poof up everywhere); mix until combined. Reduce speed to low and slowly add cocoa mixture and vanilla until incorporated. Pour into prepared pans.

4. Bake 35 to 40 minutes, or until a toothpick inserted into the center comes out with just a few crumbs on it. Mom says that if the cakes start pulling away from the pans, you should take them out of the oven or they'll be dry. Let cakes cool in pans 10 to 15 minutes. Flip onto wire racks to cool at least 1 hour before stacking (with a thin layer of frosting between) and frosting the sides and top.

Frostings and Toppings

B ecause a cake without frosting is like a sky without stars. These decadent frostings can top chocolate cake (page 138) or make any box mix special.

Basic Cream-Cheese Frosting: With an electric mixer on medium-high speed, beat 1 stick (½ cup) room-temperature unsalted butter and 1 (8-ounce) package room-temperature cream cheese until smooth. Mix in ½ teaspoon vanilla extract. Gradually add 2 cups powdered sugar. (Taste and adjust as necessary.)

Coconut Cream-Cheese Frosting: Prepare as above, then stir ½ teaspoon coconut extract into frosting. After frosting cake, garnish all over with shredded coconut. For romantic occasions, adding pink flowers around the serving dish doesn't hurt.

Chocolate Frosting: Melt 1 stick (½ cup) unsalted butter; add 1 teaspoon vanilla extract. Mix in ½ cup cocoa powder and 3 cups powdered sugar. Add ¼ cup milk and whisk until smooth and shiny.

Peanut Butter Frosting: Beat 2 cups powdered sugar, 1½ cups creamy peanut butter, ½ cup room-temperature unsalted butter, ¼ cup whole milk, and ½ teaspoon vanilla extract on medium-high speed until fluffy and creamy. Top with chopped peanut-butter-cup candies.

Other easy cake toppings include pudding (banana, butterscotch, chocolate, mint, vanilla) and plain ol' whipped cream.

Metric Conversion Chart

Volume

U.S.	Metric
¼ tsp	1.25 ml
½ tsp	2.5 ml
1 tsp	5 ml
1 tbsp (3 tsp)	15 ml
1 fl oz (2 tbsp)	30 ml
¼ cup	60 ml
⅓ cup	80 ml
½ cup	120 ml
1 cup	240 ml
1 pint (2 cups)	480 ml
1 quart (2 pints)	960 ml
1 gallon (4 quarts)	3.84 liters

Weight

U.S.	Metric
1 oz	28 g
4 oz (¼ lb)	113 g
8 oz (½ lb)	227 g
12 oz (¾ lb)	340 g
16 oz (1 lb)	454 g
2.2 lb	1 kg

Length

Inches	Centimeters
¼	0.65
½	1.25
1	2.50
2	5.00
3	7.50
4	10.0
5	12.5

Oven Temperature

Degrees Fahrenheit	Degrees Centigrade	British Gas Marks
200	93	—
250	120	½
275	140	1
300	150	2
325	165	3
350	175	4
375	190	5
400	200	6
450	230	8

irreference \ir-'ef-(ə-)rən(t)s\ n (2009)

1 : irreverent reference
2 : real information that also entertains or amuses

How-Tos. Quizzes. Instructions.
Recipes. Crafts. Jokes.
Trivia. Games. Tricks.
Quotes. Advice. Tips.

Learn something. Or not.

VISIT IRREFERENCE.COM
The New Quirk Books Web Site